S0-ATP-369

TOP 10
HOCKEY
SCORERS

Ron Knapp

SPORTS
TOP 10

ENSLOW PUBLISHERS, INC.

Bloy St. & Ramsey Ave.	P.O. Box 38
Box 777	Aldershot
Hillside, N.J. 07205	Hants GU12 6BP
U.S.A.	U.K.

Library of Congress Cataloging-in-Publication Data

Knapp, Ron.
      Top ten hockey scorers / by Ron Knapp.
         p. cm.—(Sports top ten)
      Includes bibliographical references and index.
      ISBN 0-89490-517-1
      1. Hockey players—Biography—Juvenile literature. 2. Hockey—
Records—Juvenile literature. [1. Hockey players. 2. Hockey—
Records.] I. Title. II. Title: Top 10 hockey scorers.
III. Series.
GV848.A1K63   1994
796.962'092'2—dc20
   [B]   94-1317
                                            CIP
                                          AC

Printed in the United States of America

10 9 8 7 6 5 4 3 2 1

Photo Credits: Hockey Hall of Fame, p. 17; Imperial Oil Turofsky Collection/Hockey
Hall of Frame, p. 15; Mitchell Layton, pp. 10, 13; Doug MacLellan/ Hockey Hall of Fame,
pp. 22, 25, 31, 33; Miles Nadal/Hockey Hall of Fame, p. 29; Frank Prazak/Hockey Hall
of Fame, pp. 6, 9, 19, 21, 26, 34, 37, 38, 41, 43, 45.

Cover Photo: Doug MacLellan/Hockey Hall of Fame.

Interior Design: Richard Stalzer.

CONTENTS

INTRODUCTION

HOCKEY'S GREATEST SCORERS DON'T ALL fit the same mold. Some of them were big and strong. Others relied on speed and passing. Some tried to intimidate their opponents with nasty looks, hard checks, or their fists. But Wayne Gretzky, the man with more points than anybody, has been compared to a feather.

Most of the great scorers have been forwards, the ones who skate nearest their opponents' goals. Phil Esposito loved to stand right in front of the net, slamming in shot after shot. But Bobby Orr earned his reputation as an offensive threat when he was a defenseman.

Toughness is probably the only trait they all share. Players get slashed, punched, and checked every time they skate onto the ice. The great scorers spend their careers wrapped in bandages, getting stitched up, and picking their teeth up off the ice. You have to be tough to keep coming back from that kind of punishment.

What kind of a player stays on the ice and wins a game when he's so dizzy he can barely skate? Maurice Richard did.

What kind of a player comes back after almost dying on the ice from a brain injury, then plays another thirty years? Gordie Howe did.

What kind of a player fights off cancer for two months, returns to his team right from the hospital, then wins a scoring title? Mario Lemieux did.

In most sports, the scorers are the most popular, exciting players. And it is no different in hockey. These scorers have rooms full of the trophies the National Hockey League gives to its heroes. Altogether, the ten athletes in this book have won the Ross Trophy thirty-five times. It's awarded each season to the player with the most points—the total of his goals and assists. They've taken the Hart Memorial Trophy for most valuable player thirty times.

But most important, these great scorers made their teams great. They've played on twenty-seven Stanley Cup–winning teams.

CAREER STATISTICS

Player	NHL Seasons	Games	Goals	Assists	Points
PHIL ESPOSITO	18	1282	717	873	1590
WAYNE GRETZKY	15	1125	803	1655	2458
GORDIE HOWE	26	1767	801	1049	1850
BOBBY HULL	16	1063	610	560	1170
BRETT HULL	8	540	413	287	700
GUY LAFLEUR	17	1126	560	793	1353
MARIO LEMIEUX	10	599	494	717	1211
STAN MIKITA	22	1394	541	926	1467
BOBBY ORR	12	657	270	645	915
MAURICE RICHARD	18	978	544	421	965

PHIL ESPOSITO

Phil Esposito set an NHL record by scoring 76 goals in the 1970–1971 season. The record stood until 1982 when Wayne Gretzky scored 92.

WHEN HE WAS WITH THE Boston Bruins, Phil Esposito was the most dangerous center in the NHL. He planted himself in front of the opposition's goalie and took his shots. He would be bumped and hooked and slashed but he never moved. He just stood there and kept shooting. "I see him taking all those shots," said Montreal goalie Ken Dryden, "and I wonder why his arms don't fall off."[1]

Growing up in Sault Ste. Marie, Ontario, Canada, Phil was a big boy, but not a very good athlete. When he was in elementary school, he couldn't make the school hockey team. In high school, his football team didn't win a game. "I liked being a linebacker," he said, "probably because I loved to tackle guys."[2]

But his hockey skills improved enough so that by 1964 he had earned a spot with the Chicago Black Hawks. In his first game, he never even took a shot. But he soon discovered that scoring wasn't his job with the Black Hawks. His job was to get the puck to Bobby Hull, the man who was supposed to get the goals. In Esposito's last year with Chicago (1966–1967), he only scored 27 goals.

All that changed when he joined Bobby Orr on the Bruins. In his second year with Boston (1968–1969), he became the first NHL player to break the 100-point barrier—49 goals, 77 assists, for a total of 126 points. The next year, Orr beat him 120 points to 99 points. Together they led the Bruins to a Stanley Cup championship.

For the next four seasons Esposito went on a scoring frenzy, winning the Ross Trophy with 152, 133, 130, and 145 points. The next season he had 127, but he was beaten by Orr's 135.

In 1972, the Bruins again took the Stanley Cup. That year Esposito led Team Canada in a six-game series against the former Union of Soviet Socialist Republics. He was the top scorer with 7 goals and 6 assists, and the Canadian stars won 4 games, lost 3, and tied 1.

Early in the 1975–1976 season, Esposito was traded to the New York Rangers. At that point, he had six of the top seven point-scoring seasons in NHL history. He also had the five highest goal totals. When he retired in 1981, his 717 regular season goals and 1,590 points were second only to Gordie Howe.

Today Phil Esposito is remembered best for his years with the Bruins, one of the most explosive and dominating teams in hockey history. In the 1970–1971 season, Boston had the top four scorers in the league: Esposito, 152; Orr, 139; Johnny Bucyk, 116; and Kenny Hodge, 105. Some retired players complained that the Bruins only did so well because they were playing a longer season in an expanded league against weaker players. Esposito didn't believe that for a minute. He said, "I think there's never been a hockey club that could tie our skate laces."[3]

Phil Esposito

BORN: February 20, 1942, Saulte Ste. Marie, Ontario, Canada.

PRO: Chicago Black Hawks, 1963–1967; Boston Bruins, 1967–1975; New York Rangers, 1975–1981.

POSITION: Center.

RECORDS: First NHL player to score 100 points in a season.

HONORS: NHL Scoring Leader, 1969, 1971–1974. Hart Memorial Trophy (NHL MVP), 1969, 1974. Hockey Hall of Fame, 1984.

In 1972 Phil Esposito led Team Canada, a team of NHL all-stars, to victory over the former Soviet Union's national hockey team.

WAYNE GRETZKY

Wayne Gretzky has come to be known as "The Great One." With nearly every major NHL record under his belt, he is a legend in his own time.

WALTER GRETZKY TOLD HIS YOUNG son, "Wayne, keep practicing and one day you're gonna have so many trophies, we're not gonna have room for them all."[1] He was right. By the time Wayne was ten years old, he had won a youth league scoring championship. He had 378 goals in a 69-game season. That was 238 more than any other player.

Gretzky continued collecting trophies after he joined the NHL. By the end of the 1992–1993 season, he had won nine Hart trophies, nine Ross trophies, two Conn Smythe trophies, and three Lady Byng Memorial trophies.

"Don't get bigheaded on me," Wayne's father also told him. "No matter how good you are, there's always someone better."[2] Today there are many who would argue with Mr. Gretzky. There has never been a hockey player like "The Great One." When he was 19 years old, he became the youngest player ever to have a 50-goal season. And he had 51 goals in the 1979–1980 season. A year later he set records with 109 assists, for a total of 164 points.

Then in 1981–1982, he had what was probably the greatest season in the history of hockey. In his first 39 games, he scored 50 goals. He ended that spree with 9 goals in 2 games, 4 against Los Angeles and 5 against Philadelphia. "I ate breakfast with Wayne both mornings," said his teammate Paul Coffey. "He looked at me both days and said, 'I think I'll get four or five goals today.' He said it like, 'I'm going to get more eggs.' It was something I'll never forget."[3] By the end of the season, he had 92 goals and 212 points.

The Great One had begun his total domination of the scoring statistics. He led the NHL in scoring for seven consecutive seasons (1981–1987). For eight straight years (1980–1987), he was the league's Most Valuable Player.

Gretzky led the Edmonton Oilers to four Stanley Cups in ten years. In 1989 he joined the Los Angeles Kings. That year, he became the NHL's all-time leading scorer when he passed Gordie Howe's total of 1,850 points. Early in the 1990–1991 season, he became the first player to score 2,000.

Late in the 1993–1994 season, he passed Howe's record of 801 NHL career goals. His achievement brought him a lot of attention, but he had other things on his mind. "He hasn't talked much about the record . . ." said his wife, Janet Jones. "Right now, he's more concerned with winning the games."[4] He was very disappointed that season when the Kings didn't even make the playoffs.

It isn't size or speed or strength that makes Gretzky great. He was only 4 feet 4 inches tall and 70 pounds when he scored 378 goals as a 10-year-old. Today he's only 5 feet 11 inches tall and 170 pounds. There are plenty of bigger players who skate faster and shoot harder.

Gretzky is great because he has never forgotten another piece of advice from his father: "Skate to where the puck's going to be, not to where it has been."[5] He has superb reflexes and the ability to anticipate where the puck and his opponents are going. Gretzky always seems a step ahead of everybody else on the ice. His opponents can only try to keep up with him. And, as his former teammate Dennis Sobchuk pointed out, "Ever try to catch a feather? That's what Wayne is like."[6]

WAYNE GRETZKY

BORN: January 26, 1961, Brantford, Ontario, Canada.

PRO: Indianapolis Racers, 1978; Edmonton Oilers, 1978–1988; Los Angeles Kings, 1988– .

POSITION: Center.

RECORDS: All-time leader in points, assists and goals.

HONORS: Hart Memorial Trophy (NHL MVP), 1980–1987, 1989.
NHL Scoring Leader, 1981–1987, 1990–1991, 1994.
Lady Byng Memorial Trophy, 1980, 1991–1992.

Before leaving the Edmonton Oilers, Gretzky helped lead them to four Stanley Cup championships.

GORDIE HOWE

AS A BIG, SHY KID in Saskatoon, Saskatchewan, Canada, Gordie Howe spent most of his time at the hockey rink. His family wasn't rich, so his first skates were second hand. His sticks were broken ones other players had thrown away. He stuffed magazines into his socks for pads.

Howe joined the Detroit Red Wings in 1946 when he was eighteen years old. His career almost ended during the 1950 Stanley Cup playoffs when he crashed headfirst into the boards. Unfortunately, that was before players wore helmets. His face was covered with blood. He was carried from the ice and rushed to the hospital. His skull had cracked, and his brain was swelling from the injury. Doctors operated immediately to save his life.

Even with Gordie Howe in the hospital, the Red Wings won the Stanley Cup that year. Howe's head injury healed and he got back in the game. The Red Wings went on to take the Cup three times in the next five seasons. Then Maurice Richard led the rival Montreal Canadiens to five Cups in a row; he retired after the last one in 1960.

By then, Richard had 544 regular season goals, more than anybody else. Canadiens' fans hoped that record would last forever. They believed that "The Rocket" was the game's greatest player. They forgot that Gordie Howe was still on the ice, and he was picking up about 30 goals a year. By November 10, 1963, he was just one short of Richard's record, and Detroit was playing Montreal. The Canadiens concentrated on stopping Howe. They bumped and checked him and kept

GORDIE HOWE

Gordie Howe played for an amazing 32 seasons in the NHL and WHA. He was named MVP six times between 1952 and 1963.

the puck far away from him. The strategy almost worked. Howe got only two shots all night, but he knocked the second one past goalie Gump Worsley to tie Richard's record.

Two weeks later, the two teams met again. On a power play, the Red Wings were a man short and the entire Canadiens squad was trying to stop Howe. He took a pass from Billy McNeill and slapped the puck into the net. The Canadiens players skated quietly to the bench and the Detroit crowd stood and cheered for seven minutes.

So, early in his eighteenth season, Howe had more goals than anybody. But he didn't stop there. He just kept playing . . . and playing . . . and playing. After twenty-five years with the Red Wings, he retired in 1971. He had a total of 787 goals. But two years later, he joined the Houston Aeros in the new World Hockey Association (WHA) so that he could play on the same team with his sons Mark and Marty. In his first season there, he scored 31 goals and 69 assists, and earned the league's MVP award. Not bad for a forty-seven-year-old.

Gordie Howe scored 369 points in his 4 years with the Aeros. After two seasons with New England in the WHA, he signed with the Hartford Whalers, a new team in the NHL. He was fifty-two years old in his last season (1979–1980), but he still played all eighty games.

Gordie Howe finally retired for good after thirty-two years as a pro. He had 975 regular season goals with 801 in the NHL. No other athlete in any sport has ever had a career to match his. His records were finally erased by Wayne Gretzky many years later.

The former prime minister of Canada, Lester B. Pearson, said Gordie Howe "has earned the title: Mr. Hockey."[1] Even Maurice Richard was forced to admit, "Howe was a better all-around player than I was."[2]

GORDIE HOWE

BORN: March 31, 1928, Floral, Saskatchewan, Canada.

PRO: Detroit Red Wings, 1946–1971; Houston Aeros, 1973–1977;
New England, 1977–1979; Hartford Whalers, 1979–1980.

POSITION: Right Wing.

RECORDS: NHL Games played, 1,767; NHL Seasons played, 26.

HONORS: NHL Scoring Leader, 1951–1954, 1957, 1963.
Hart Memorial Trophy (NHL MVP), 1952, 1953, 1957, 1958,
1960, 1963. Hockey Hall of Fame, 1972.

Gordie Howe held the most NHL career records until the arrival of
Wayne Gretzky. He is now second in points, goals and assists.

BOBBY HULL

WHEN HE WAS A CHILD on the family farm in Ontario, Canada, one of Bobby Hull's jobs was to chop wood. He didn't know it then, but chopping wood builds up arm muscles. By the time he was a star with the Chicago Black Hawks, Hull's biceps measured seventeen and one-half inches. That was even bigger than those of Muhammad Ali, who was then the heavyweight boxing champion of the world.

But young Bobby did more in Ontario than just chop wood. He had learned to skate when he was just three years old. By the time he was twelve, he was big enough and strong enough to play hockey on an adult team with his father.

When he was a superstar in the NHL, the "Golden Jet" used his massive arm muscles to shoot the puck harder than anybody. His slapshots were clocked at almost 120 miles per hour.

But Hull had more than power. He was also the fastest player on the ice—he could skate close to 30 miles per hour. When he shot, he didn't always try to blast the puck. He used a curved blade on his heavy stick to fling pucks at the net like he was using a slingshot.

Bobby Hull won his first NHL scoring title during the 1959–1960 season, when he was only twenty-one years old. The next year he led the Black Hawks to their first Stanley Cup since 1938. Until the 1961–1962 season, only two play-ers—Maurice "The Rocket" Richard and Bernie "Boom Boom" Geoffrion—had ever scored 50 goals in a season. That year Hull should have had 51, but one of his goals was given

Bobby Hull is kept in check. His shots were known to travel nearly 120 miles per hour.

BOBBY HULL

to another player by mistake. Bobby never complained. Fans liked his attitude. They also liked the friendly way he treated the thousands of people who wanted his autograph.

Hull was a nice guy, but he was also tough. Just before the 1963 playoffs with Detroit, he suffered a separated shoulder. He played anyway—and scored two goals in the first game. Then in the next game his nose was smashed and broken. He came back to finish the series with a pair of black eyes looking over a splinted, bandaged nose. And he scored a hat trick in the last game.

In the 1965–1966 season, he scored 44 goals in his first 45 games. He cooled off the next year, but he still got 54 goals for the whole season. He got 52 the next year, then 58 in the 1968–1969 season.

In 1972, Bobby Hull became the first major player to join the new World Hockey Association. He got a million dollars to leave the Black Hawks and join the Winnipeg Jets. When he switched leagues and signed a huge contract, he changed the way hockey was run. Now the NHL owners had to compete against the WHA for athletes. Salaries shot upward. For the first time, hockey players made big money.

Hull's greatest season with the Jets was 1974–1975. He scored 77 goals in just 78 games. Winnipeg won the Avco World Trophy as WHA champions the next season and again in the 1977–1978 season.

Bobby Hull is still remembered fondly in Chicago and Winnipeg even years after his retirement. And today's players still realize how much they owe the Golden Jet. As his Black Hawk teammate Stan Mikita pointed out, "After all he's done for all of us, all we should do is bow whenever he walks into the room and kiss his feet."[1]

BOBBY HULL

BORN: January 3, 1939, Pointe Anne, Ontario, Canada.

PRO: Chicago Black Hawks, 1957–1972; Winnipeg Jets, 1972–1980; Hartford Whalers, 1980.

POSITION: Left Wing.

HONORS: NHL Scoring Leader, 1960, 1962, 1966.
Hart Memorial Trophy (NHL MVP), 1965, 1966.
Lady Byng Memorial Trophy, 1965.
Hockey Hall of Fame, 1983.

Bobby Hull was nicknamed the "Golden Jet" because of his speed and blond hair.

BRETT HULL

Brett Hull amazed his detractors when he scored 86 goals in the 1990–1991 season, the third best scoring season of all time.

NOBODY SHOULD BE SURPRISED THAT Brett Hull became a hockey star. His mother, Joanne, was a professional figure skater. His father, of course, is Bobby Hull, the "Golden Jet."

But, despite his parents, the "Golden Brett" wasn't always a great hockey player. For many years he was known as a fat and lazy athlete who relied on his vicious slapshot and his famous name. In his first full season in the NHL with the Calgary Flames, he only scored 26 goals. He was pulled out of games for making mistakes or for not hustling.

In 1988 he was traded to the St. Louis Blues. He had a pretty good year—41 goals and 84 points. But the Blues' coach, Brian Sutter, thought he could do better. He told Hull that he had the skills to be a great hockey player, not just a good one. "It was up to him and how hard he wanted to work."[1]

Brett decided to take the challenge. He finally realized, "It doesn't matter a lick if you are given the ability if you don't go out and develop it."[2] During the off-season, he worked out, got in better shape, and lost ten pounds. He also spent hundreds of hours on the ice, improving his wrist shot. By the time the 1989–1990 season began, he was a much better player. He led the league with 72 goals. That made Brett and his dad the first father-and-son combination to each have 50-goal seasons. Bobby Hull's best NHL total was 58 goals with the Chicago Black Hawks in the 1968–1969 season.

Brett was still playing great hockey the next year. He had back-to-back hat trick games. In his first 49 games, he scored 50 goals. Only Wayne Gretzky, Maurice Richard, Mario Lemieux, and Mike Bossy had ever gotten 50 goals in 50 or fewer games. When the regular season ended, he had 86, the third-highest total ever. He was awarded the Hart Memorial Trophy as the league's most valuable player (MVP).

The Blues met the Minnesota North Stars in the second round of the 1991 playoffs. To beat St. Louis, the North Stars knew they had to stop Brett. They decided to assign two players to "shadow" him through the series. The strategy worked. Hull got only 3 goals, and the Blues lost the series— four games to two.

The "Golden Brett" has a reputation as one of the league's most precise shooters. He's an expert at hitting the corners of the net. Because he shoots so quickly and hits the puck so hard, goalies have little time to get ready for his shots. "You can't give him any openings to shoot at," said former Detroit Red Wing goalie Tim Cheveldae. "He'll get the puck there before you know it."[3]

Other goalies get nervous when Hull is on the ice. They agree with Sutter, who said Brett is a "scary" player. "He shoots so hard, the puck jumps and zips. It's like a cannon shot."[4]

BRETT HULL

BORN: August 9, 1964, Belleville, Ontario, Canada.

PRO: Calgary Flames, 1987–1988; St. Louis Blues, 1988– .

POSITION: Right Wing.

RECORDS: Right Wing Scoring Record (86 goals).

HONORS: Hart Memorial Trophy (NHL MVP), 1991.

Like his dad, the "Golden Jet," Brett Hull also has a killer slap shot.

GUY LAFLEUR

Guy Lafleur dominated the NHL in the late 1970s. He led the league in scoring (1976–1978) and was twice named league MVP.

TWO HOURS BEFORE EVERY GAME Guy Lafleur could be found in the Montreal Canadiens' locker room, slamming hockey sticks against a table. "If you aren't expecting it," said teammate Ken Dryden, "that sound really makes you jump."[1] "The Flower" was settling his nerves before hitting the ice. He was also looking for sticks that wouldn't crack.

Even on the ice he made nasty sounds with his stick. In a game in 1976 against the Buffalo Sabres, his teammate Yvan Cournoyer flipped a long pass from beside the Sabres' net. The puck was sailing toward the blue line and out of play. Lafleur streaked across the ice and slapped the puck back at the net. The shot came so fast and so hard that goalie Gerry Desjardins said, "I never had a chance to move. Anyway it was one of those shots that I'm almost glad I didn't get a piece of. It would have hurt for a week."[2]

In Boston, fans still talk about the great shot that killed the Bruins in the 1979 semifinals. Late in the game, Lafleur got the puck near his own goalie and took off. At the blue line, he passed ahead to teammate Jacques Lemaire. Together they closed in on the Bruin goalie. Lemaire flipped the puck back and Guy raised his stick behind him, winding up for a slap shot. Without even stopping the puck, he shot it on a line into the net.

When Guy Lafleur was a teenager, he was the best junior player in Canada, scoring 130 goals in his last season with the Quebec Ramparts. He was drafted by the Montreal Canadiens in 1971. He was expected to be one of the biggest stars in the NHL, but in his first three years, he never scored more than 29 goals. Then, in the 1974–1975 season, his pro career finally took off. He got 53 goals for a total of 66 points.

That was the first of 6 straight 50-goal seasons for The Flower. While he was with the Canadiens, they won five Stanley Cups, four of them in a row (1975–1979). Lafleur's 125 points won the Ross Trophy for the 1975–1976 season, and helped Montreal win 58 regular season games, a league record. He scored 17 more in the playoffs. The Canadiens were even tougher the next year. Guy took the Ross Trophy again with 136 points, and the team won 60 games. He won both the Ross and Hart trophies for the 1977–1978 season with 60 goals. This was the best total of his career.

Montreal was dominating the NHL, but it was hardly a one-man effort. For instance, in the 1976–1977 season, he was one of four Canadiens on the six-man first All-Star team. Lafleur and Steve Shutt were the wings, Dryden was the goalie, and Larry Robinson was a defenseman. The strength of the team helped Lafleur's totals. He finished his career with 560 regular season goals.

The Canadiens were a great team, but the biggest star was always the man his fans called "Superfleur." According to *Hockey Hall of Fame: The Official History of the Game and Its Greatest Stars*, "Lafleur was the NHL's most compelling player, combining superior speed with a hard, accurate shot and a dazzling array of improvisational moves."[3]

GUY LAFLEUR

BORN: September 20, 1951, Montreal, Quebec, Canada.

PRO: Montreal Canadiens, 1971– 1985; New York Rangers, 1988–1989; Quebec Nordiques, 1989–1991.

POSITION: Right Wing.

HONORS: Three-time NHL Scoring Leader, 1975–78.

Hart Memorial Trophy (NHL MVP), 1977, 1978.

Hockey Hall of Fame, 1988.

Lafleur was not just an individual star. He helped lead the Canadiens to five championships.

IN FRENCH, *LE MIEUX* MEANS "the best." Wayne Gretzky feels Mario Lemieux deserves the name. In fact, "The Great One" (Gretzky) said, "Mario could end up as the greatest ever."[1] If he stays healthy, maybe Lemieux will be the man who rewrites Gretzky's scoring records.

In the 1987–1988 season, Mario Lemieux was the first player in seven years to take a scoring title from Gretzky. He was also named the Hart Memorial Trophy (MVP) winner, breaking an eight-year Gretzky streak.

Early in his career Mario chose "66" as his number, flipping The Great One's "99." But Gretzky wasn't his only hockey hero. When Lemieux was growing up near Montreal, Quebec, Canada, he copied the style of Guy Lafleur, the great Montreal Canadien star. In his last season as a junior player, he scored 282 points in seventy games.

But Lemieux has had to overcome injuries and other health problems during his career. For instance, during the 1989 playoffs with the Philadelphia Flyers he had a severely sprained neck. This kept him even from skating in the pregame warmups. But when the game began, he was on the ice with his Pittsburgh Penguin teammates. Just a little over two minutes into the game, he backhanded a shot past the Flyer goalie. Less than two minutes later, he deflected a pass into the net. Three minutes after that he slapped another one in. It had taken him less than seven minutes to get a hat trick. Before the game was over, he had 2 more goals. Pittsburgh had won, 10–3.

Lemieux was in bed for two months after back surgery in 1990. Eight months later, painful back spasms forced him to

MARIO LEMIEUX

Before Mario Lemieux arrived, the Penguins had never even been to a Stanley Cup championship. Now their name has been engraved on the cup twice.

sit out the third game of the Stanley Cup finals against the Minnesota North Stars. In the next game, though, he got a goal and an assist. The Penguins evened the series with a 5–3 win. After another 6–4 victory, Lemieux's team won the Cup with a smashing 8–0 win. A year later, he led the Penguins to a finals sweep over the Chicago Black Hawks and another Stanley Cup. He had played with a broken hand!

Then early in 1993, Lemieux faced his greatest challenge. He was diagnosed with Hodgkin's disease, a form of cancer. He stayed away from hockey for two months while doctors attacked the cancer with radiation therapy. As soon as the treatments ended, he was back on the ice—just in time to win his third straight scoring title. "It's amazing," said Bill Dineen, coach of the Flyers. "Obviously, his heart is in the game of hockey. You've got to give him credit for playing the way he did. You've got to give him credit for showing up."[2]

When he's healthy, Mario Lemieux is one of hockey's most exciting superstars. He's big (6 feet 4 inches tall, 210 pounds), but he moves like a small forward. He gets around the ice quickly. And he can put the moves on with his stickhandling and his skating. He is also an excellent passer.

"I grew up watching Bobby Orr," said Pittsburgh's Kevin Stevens. "And Wayne Gretzky was phenomenal. But Mario is on another level."[3]

Mario Lemieux

Born: October 5, 1965, Montreal, Quebec, Canada.

Pro: Pittsburgh Penguins, 1984– .

Position: Center.

Records: NHL highest goals per game average, 1.827.

Honors: NHL Scoring Leader, 1988, 1989, 1992, 1993.
Calder Memorial Trophy (Rookie of the Year), 1985.
Hart Memorial Trophy (NHL MVP), 1988, 1993.

Mario Lemieux is probably the greatest star in the NHL today. If his health holds out, he may end up being the greatest of all time.

STAN MIKITA

Le Petit Diable's intensity on the ice made him a favorite with the fans.

AT FIRST GLANCE, STAN MIKITA didn't look like a hockey player. He was only 5 feet 9 inches tall and weighed 170 pounds. But his opponents knew better. They had seen the size of his arms and wrists. Doing a hundred pushups a day gave Mikita two of the strongest arms in the game. He was also tough. During the 1961–1962 season, he played with two broken toes. "Once I took off my skates between periods," he said, "and they were filled with blood."[1] Of course he laced them up again and returned to the ice.

When Mikita was eight, his family moved from his native Czechoslovakia to St. Catherines, Ontario. One of the first words he learned in his new country was "puck." At first, some of his Canadian classmates made fun of his accent and his inability to understand them. Since he was so small, they thought he would be easy to push around. They soon discovered their mistake. Young Stan was willing to stand up for himself and fight if necessary. He was small, but he was tough. He also gained a reputation as a fine hockey player. When he wasn't on the rink, he enjoyed soccer, lacrosse, and baseball.

Stan was also earning a reputation as a fine soccer player. It wasn't unusual for him to score five or ten goals a game. He was also skilled at lacrosse and baseball. But he gave them all up for hockey. He got up every day at 5 A.M., so he could practice two hours before school. When he was just thirteen, a Black Hawk scout spotted him playing in a junior league.

Six years later, when he was nineteen, Mikita was playing center for the Chicago Black Hawks in the NHL. Because of his size, the other players tried to push him around. Once again he fought back. He spent 119 minutes in the penalty box when he was a rookie in the 1959–1960 season. He earned the nickname "Le Petit Diable," or "Little Devil."

Mikita soon became one of the top scorers in the league. He won the Ross Trophy as the league's top scorer two years in a row (1964 and 1965). But his penalty minutes for those seasons were 149 and 154.

The Little Devil soon decided that he liked scoring goals more than getting penalties. He cut back on his penalty time by not retaliating when he was bumped or slashed by opponents. Instead of being tough, he tried to stick to his speedy skating and powerful shooting. Bobby Hull, his Chicago teammate, said he had become the smartest player in the game.

Mikita's new style paid off. In the 1966–1967 season, he only got twelve minutes of penalty time. He was awarded the Lady Byng Memorial Trophy for his sportsmanship and skill. More importantly he won another Ross Trophy with 97 points. He was also voted the Hart Memorial Trophy as the NHL's most valuable player. It was the first time anybody had ever won the Lady Byng, Ross, and Hart trophies in the same year. The next season he took all the trophies again with 87 points and just 14 minutes in penalties.

Mikita had a reputation for getting goals when his team needed them the most. In just twelve games in the 1962 Stanley Cup Playoffs, for instance, he set a record—21 points from 6 goals and 15 assists. As goalie Gump Worsley said, "Mikita, he'll always make the big plays that'll kill you."[2]

STAN MIKITA

BORN: May 20, 1940, Czechoslovakia.

PRO: Chicago Black Hawks, 1959–1980.

POSITION: Center.

HONORS: NHL Scoring Leader, 1964, 1965, 1967, 1968.

Hart Memorial Trophy (NHL MVP), 1967, 1968.

Lady Byng Memorial Trophy, 1967, 1968.

Hockey Hall of Fame, 1983.

Though Mikita was known for his toughness, he later won two Lady Byng trophies. The award is given out each year to the league's "most gentlemanly player."

BOBBY ORR

Bobby Orr broke all NHL records as a defenseman. No one since has excelled at both defense and offense in quite the same way.

THE FOURTH GAME OF THE Stanley Cup finals was tied 3–3 in overtime. All the Boston Bruins needed was one goal to win their first title in twenty-nine years. Bobby Orr skated toward the St. Louis Blues' net with the puck. The St. Louis defenders closed in. Orr passed the puck off to teammate Derek Sanderson, who knocked it right back. Then, just before he was flattened by a hard check, Orr slapped the puck past the Blues' goalie. The Bruins won, 4–3! The Boston Garden crowd swarmed onto the ice to mob the man they called "Bobby Hockey."

Orr wasn't just another exciting high-scoring forward. He was a defenseman who changed the way the game was played. Until Bobby arrived, defensemen were usually big but slow skaters who hardly ever shot. Orr played the position almost like he was an extra forward. He liked to use his speed and shooting ability to score goals, too.

Bobby Orr scored a lot of points, but he always remembered that his first job was to keep the other team from scoring. He played hard, and he was all over the ice. When Bobby Hull was checked by Orr, Hull said it felt like being hit by a truck.

After losing the puck to Bobby, an opponent complained, "That's no defenseman. That's a commando raid."[1]

Orr was so good he was first spotted by pro scouts when he was just twelve. By the time he was fifteen, he was outplaying twenty-year-olds in Canada's top junior league.

Bobby became the first defenseman to lead the league in scoring. He was also the first to get more than 100 points in a season. In 1967, he was the Calder Memorial Trophy winner as Rookie of the Year. Three years later, he became the first player to win *four* NHL trophies in a single season—Hart (regular season MVP), James Norris (best defenseman), Ross (most points), and Conn Smythe (playoff MVP). That year he was also named *Sports Illustrated*'s Sportsman of the Year.

In his last complete season (1974–1975), Bobby scored 46 goals, his best total. He also won his second Ross Trophy. The next year he was only able to play ten regular season games. He was still named to Team Canada in 1976 for the Canada Cup tournament, though. His team beat Czechoslovakia in the title game, and he was named tournament MVP.

At his peak, Orr was in magnificent shape. It wasn't unusual for him to be on the ice for 65 percent of the game. And while he was there he was all over the rink. Even skating backwards he could keep up with almost any forward.

Throughout his career, Orr was bothered by bad knees. By 1978, he had eight Norris trophies, three Hart trophies, and six knee operations. He realized that his knees were no longer strong enough for him to play professional hockey. He reluctantly retired.

In Boston, "Bobby Hockey" is still revered as one of the most popular players ever to step on the ice. His first Bruins coach, Harry Sinden, said, "Bobby was a star from the moment they played the National Anthem in his first NHL game."[2]

BOBBY ORR

BORN: March 20, 1948, Parry Sound, Ontario, Canada.

PRO: Boston Bruins, 1966–1976; Chicago Black Hawks, 1976–1978.

POSITION: Defenseman.

RECORDS: Most goals by a defenseman (career), 270.

HONORS: Norris Trophy winner, 1968–1975.
NHL scoring leader, 1970, 1975.
Hart Memorial Trophy (NHL MVP), 1970–1972.
Calder Memorial Trophy (Rookie of the Year), 1967.

A knee injury forced Orr to retire in 1978, prematurely ending his career at age thirty.

MAURICE RICHARD

A HARD CHECK SENT MAURICE Richard into the boards and bloodied his head. That should have been enough to send him to the hospital. But "The Rocket" was anxious to get back on the ice. After all, it was the deciding game of the 1952 Stanley Cup finals. Instead of heading for the hospital, he ended up in the Montreal Canadiens' locker room. He spent the second period getting his head stitched up there.

So, despite the stitches and a terrible headache, he was ready to play in the third period. "I was dizzy and a few times when I got the puck I didn't know whether I was skating toward our goal or their goal," he said.[1] But with four minutes left he slipped past four Boston Bruins to make the winning shot.

The Rocket was a superb athlete. As a youngster, he was a great wrestler, boxer, and baseball player. Lucky for the Canadiens, hockey was the sport he loved the most.

Richard was a fierce competitor who checked hard and played rough. Some of his opponents said he was a dirty player. He did get more than his share of penalty minutes, but he never changed his style of play.

He loved to win. "When we lost," said his teammate Jean Beliveau, "the Rocket did not need to say anything to show how hard he accepted defeat. You could see it in his eyes."[2]

He was almost impossible to stop. Sometimes he skated right into defensemen. He carried them on his back up to the goal line where he popped the puck into the net. In the 1944 Stanley Cup playoffs, the Toronto Maple Leafs assigned Bob Davidson to "shadow" Richard. Davidson's job was to chase The Rocket up and down the ice, checking him every chance

MAURICE RICHARD

Maurice Richard became the only NHL player to score 50 goals in the old 50-game season in 1944–1945.

he got. "Sometimes he stayed so close to me that I got angry," Maurice said, "and that night, I guess, I took it out on him—and the puck."[3] He got a hat trick (3 goals) in the second period, then 2 more in the third. Those 5 goals were a Stanley Cup record.

Sometimes two players were assigned to shadow him. That didn't bother The Rocket, either. He enjoyed skating into them, then glaring down at them as they laid on the ice.

In the 1944–1945 season, he became the first player to score 50 goals. And that was when there were only fifty games in the season! One day that year, he was a little tired after spending the day moving into a new home. But he still scored 5 goals and 3 assists in the game that night!

Richard's temper caused serious trouble in 1955. He slashed a Boston Bruin with his stick, then slugged one of the officials. The fight soon turned into a riot that spilled out of the Montreal Forum onto the nearby streets. The Canadiens had to forfeit the game, and Richard was suspended.

Probably no hockey player has ever aroused such fear in his opponents. Goalies dreaded the sight of The Rocket blasting down the ice toward them. He didn't glide. He dug his skates into the ice and ran like a sprinter. "When he came flying toward you with the puck on his stick," said goalie Glenn Hall, "his eyes were all lit up, flashing and gleaming like a pinball machine. It was terrifying."[4]

MAURICE RICHARD

BORN: August 4, 1921, Montreal, Quebec, Canada.

PRO: Montreal Canadiens, 1942–1960.

POSITION: Right Wing.

RECORDS: First to score 50 goals in a season.

HONORS: Hart Memorial Trophy (NHL MVP), 1947.

In his eighteen-year career, Richard helped lead the Canadiens to win eight Stanley Cups.

Notes by Chapter

Phil Esposito

1. Francis Rosa, "It Doesn't Get Any Better Than This: The Big Bad Bruins," in *The Official National Hockey League 75th Anniversary Commemorative Book* (Toronto: McClelland & Stewart, Inc., 1991), p. 195.

2. Art Berke (editor-in-chief), *Lincoln Library of Sports Champions*, vol. 5 (Columbus, Ohio: Frontier Press Company, 1985), p. 92.

3. "An Orgy of Scores," *Newsweek* (April 5, 1971), p. 61.

Wayne Gretzky

1. Wayne Gretzky, with Rick Reilly, *Gretzky: An Autobiography* (New York: Harper Paperbacks, 1990), p. 20.

2. Ibid., pp. 7–8.

3. Steve Kornacki, "Gretzky Proud, Weary of Chase," *Detroit Free Press*, (March 17, 1994), p. 3D.

4. Steve Kornacki, "Gretzky Scores 2, Ties Howe at 801 Goals," *Detroit Free Press* (March 21, 1994), p. 10C.

5. Thomas R. Raber, *Wayne Gretzky: Hockey Great* (Minneapolis, Minn.: Lerner Publications Company, 1991), p. 16.

6. Zander Hollander (editor), *The Complete Encyclopedia of Hockey* (Detroit, Mich.: Visible Ink Press, 1993), p. 189.

Gordie Howe

1. Dan Diamond and Joseph Romain, *Hockey Hall of Fame: The Official History of the Game and Its Greatest Stars* (Toronto: Doubleday, 1988), p. 105.

2. Zander Hollander (editor), *The Complete Encyclopedia of Hockey* (Detroit, Mich.: Visible Ink Press, 1993), p. 191.

Bobby Hull

1. Bob Verdi, "The Golden Jet," in *The Official National Hockey League 75th Anniversary Book* (Toronto: McClelland & Stewart, Inc., 1991), p. 146.

Brett Hull

1. Margaret J. Goldstein, *Brett Hull: Hockey's Top Gun* (Minneapolis, Minn.: Lerner Publications Company, 1992), p. 22.

2. Mark Peterson, "Brett Hull: Hockey's Mr. Nice Guy," *Boys' Life* (February 1992), p. 26.

3. Ibid., p. 25.
4. Goldstein, p. 30.

Guy Lafleur

1. J. D. Reed, "The Canadiens Say It with Flowers," *Sports Illustrated* (March 22, 1976), p. 20.
2. Ibid., p. 21.
3. Dan Diamond and Joseph Romain, *Hockey Hall of Fame: The Official History of the Game and Its Greatest Stars* (Toronto: Doubleday, 1988), p. 105.

Mario Lemieux

1. Gretzky with Reilly, p. 255.
2. Joe Lapointe, "After 'A Long Two Months,' Lemieux Returns with Style," *The New York Times* (March 3, 1993), p. B17.
3. Jon Scher, "The Legend Grows," *Sports Illustrated* (April 19, 1993), p. 45.

Stan Mikita

1. William Barry Furlong, "'A Couple of Hi-hos and Here We Go,'" *Sports Illustrated* (April 30, 1962), p. 58.
2. Ibid.

Bobby Orr

1. "Hottest Man on Ice," Readers Digest (February 1971), p. 220.
2. Zander Hollander (editor), *The Complete Encyclopedia of Hockey* (Detroit, Mich.: Visible Ink Press, 1993), p. 213.

Maurice Richard

1. Hollander, p. 80.
2. Jean Beliveau, "The Heart of a Champion," in *The Official National Hockey League 75th Anniversary Commemorative Book*, p. 128.
3. Zander Hollander (editor), *The Complete Encyclopedia of Hockey* (Detroit, Mich.: Visible Ink Press, 1993), p. 257.
4. Ibid., p. 200.

INDEX

A
Ali, Muhammad, 18

B
Beliveau, Jean, 42
Bossy, Mike, 23
Bucyk, Johnny, 8

C
Cheveldae, Tim, 24
Coffey, Paul, 11
Cournoyer, Yvan, 27

D
Davidson, Bob, 42, 44
Desjardins, Gerry, 27
Dineen, Bill, 32
Dryden, Ken, 7, 27, 28

E
Esposito, Phil, 4, 5, *6*–9

G
Geoffrion, Bernie, 18
Gretzky, Walter, 11, 12
Gretzky, Wayne, 4, 5, *10*–13, 16, 23, 30, 32

H
Hall, Glenn, 44
Hodge, Kenny, 8
Howe, Gordie, 4, 5, 8, 12, 14–17
Howe, Mark, 16
Howe, Marty, 16
Hull, Bobby, 5, 7, 18–21, 23, 36, 39
Hull, Brett, 5, *22*–25
Hull, Joanne, 23

J
Jones, Janet, 12

L
Lafleur, Guy, 5, *26*–29, 30
Lemaire, Jacques, 27
Lemieux, Mario, 4, 5, 23, 30–33

M
McNeill, Billy, 16
Mikita, Stan, 5, 20, *34*–37

O
Orr, Bobby, 4, 5, 7, 8, 32, *38*–41

P
Pearson, Lester B., 16

R
Richard, Maurice, 4, 5, 14, 16, 18, 23, 42–45
Robinson, Larry, 28

S
Sanderson, Derek, 39
Shutt, Steve, 28
Sinden, Harry, 40
Sobchuk, Dennis, 12
Stanley Cup, 5, 7, 12, 14, 18, 28, 32, 36, 42
Stevens, Kevin, 32
Sutter, Brian, 23, 24

W
World Hockey Association (WHA), 16, 20
Worsley, Gump, 16, 36